Black Eyelids Etched in Gold

by

Ciderick Cumbee

and

Ashleyn Cumbee

DORRANCE
PUBLISHING CO
EST. 1920
PITTSBURGH, PENNSYLVANIA 15238

Dorrance Publishing Co
585 Alpha Drive
Suite 103
Pittsburgh, PA 15238
Visit our website at *www.dorrancebookstore.com*

ISBN: 978-1-6393-7081-8
eISBN: 978-1-6393-7869-2

This book is dedicated to ABBA,
our children and to the life of the butterfly.

Ciderick and Ashleyn Cumbee

Table of Contents

Black Eyelids Etched in Gold

Black Eyelids Etched in Gold

Black eyelids etched in gold
Black eyelids etched in gold
Black eyelids etched in gold

For you are the one that time and space foretold
Black eyelids etched in gold
An ancient bloodline of greatness and royalty
They target your inheritance with force and brutality
Black eyelids etched in gold
Black eyelids etched in gold
You are the one that the spirit foretold
Why do you think your ancestors line up to speak to you from
time to time
For you are the true spiritual power line
Black eyelids etched in gold
Black eyelids etched in gold
You are the very reason why black men love to rock the essence of gold
Why?? because of the way you stare at them with those
Black eyelids etched in gold
For even when you were pressed down into the mud of humanity
Your reflection still shone through because of those
Black eyelids etched in gold
The weight of the world you carried with your very own soul
You carried it and cradled it with every ounce of you
With that sacrificial love
You are more than worthy, you were chosen before the world was laid
Black eyelids etched in gold
Black eyelids etched in gold

You are the one that the Egyptians foretold
Black eyelids etched in gold
You are the one on the pyramid wall,
The same black eyelids carved in stone
You are Mother Nature, the true motherland

The image of the divine and the image of you walk hand in hand
Who wouldn't love to gaze upon you and those
Black eyelids etched in gold

Galaxy Queen

She wears the marks of infinity draping down her legs as she walks
by seemingly without making a move
She barely notices the trivial matters, she has her own
personal groove
Her breasts are clothed in radiance, too amazing to behold
Her mind is sharp and strong, a force that cannot be controlled
Time is draped upon her shoulders which shimmer with majesty.
Not bound by false perceptions of another's reality
Her eyes are brilliantly arrayed with eternal compassion
and motherhood
Never to be confused or separated from the strength and state of
her womanhood.
Her head bows only to the oneness from which she flowed
The one great source of everything that is bestowed.
She is a warrior, a lover, a giver, a master with value unseen
She is the galaxy queen

Her walk exudes royalty and confidence, she takes possession of
every bit of the galaxy that touches her glance
Rigel, Betelgeuse, Vegas, Alpha Andromedae marvel as she passes
by, just waiting for a chance
A chance to experience the beauty and power she exudes
Spiritual enlightenment, righteousness, loyalty imbued
She is one with creation, one with the universe, one with ABBA
That flows through the trees, the roses, the moon and the stars
that fall to worship at his feet
HE is a man of war, the ANCIENT of DAYS, a STRONG
TOWER and a loving FATHER

Who created her being and her image a smooth masterpiece
She is exquisite, an amethyst, a turquoise, a diamond, the universal Centerpiece
She is his beautiful black queen of the galaxy,
She is the Galaxy Queen

In Retrospect

Looking back on your life, searching through your database of circumstance
Remember that your failures and your letdowns are only to help you get your weight up.
Don't miss the chance to sing off key or slip and fall while attempting the latest hot dance
Count your disappointments as a stepping stone to reach the divine
It won't always look so clear and beautiful each time
Looking back in retrospect
Don't let it turn into regret

You let some people down, hurt them to their core
Betrayed the ones that meant the most to you
Rise above it, make amends, don't poison what HE has in store
No matter what you've done before, it's never too late to start your path anew
Looking back in retrospect
Don't let it turn into regret

Although your road is marred with turbulence and blame
Remember that demons are the ones who hide in your shame
So shout it out, try again, no one can fix the mess but you
Your haters came to take your shine away
But it's up to you to play the game
Remember the light you had before the world defiled you
Shout it out, turn it up, connect to the higher you
The you that shines with luminance and brilliance
The you that rises above the carnal circumstance

The you that rocks, the you that grooves and vibrates with agape
Looking back in retrospect
Don't let it turn into regret
For your time is now, the chance is here and you deserve nothing less

Good Grass

To the chocolate lookin brother with the hazel-colored skin
With the long, course dreds that hang down to his gold-plated chain
Who loves to bop his head and bite his lip to hold back that sexy grin

To the Haitian fre' with the smooth dark skin, dark and heavy on
the melanin
Who talks that talk and walks that walk, while struggling to make
a way
With the rich brown eyes, big open heart, ordained to fight since
his life began

You got that good grass, don't you know
You got that good grass fo sho
You got that good grass, it's a crown
You got that good grass, don't let the struggle hold you down

To the smooth brother with the low temp fade with spirals like the
galaxy
Who hustles hard, stacks his chips and rocks his baby to sleep
With big dreams of coming up with every opportunity

To the young, light-skinned sister with the curly coils that bounce
With the big bright smile and acoustic energy that vibrates like the sun
Who lives her life with every bit of the fire that she radiates by the
pound down to her very last ounce

You got that good grass, don't you know
You got that good grass fo sho
You got that good grass, it's a crown
You got that good grass, don't let the struggle hold you down

To the sophisticated queen that holds her hair in a wide massive bun
Who rocks the boardroom from 9 to 5 and the babies' room at night
With the deep brown skin that reacts to the power of the sun

To the dark cocoa sister who smells like shea butter with the
conditioned afro
Who stands firm even when she is alone despite all of the odds
And still shares her inner peace and love to all involved apropos

You got that good grass, don't you know
You got that good grass fo sho
You got that good grass, it's a crown
You got that good grass, don't let the struggle hold you down

Remembrance

Warm like an oven in the summertime
Like self-rising biscuits, buttered down
Soft to the core but too hot to touch
And that's why I love you so much

Sweet like that iced tea with the people gathered under the shade tree
Sweet like the lemon drop candy that the little kids play with
Even stronger than my grandfather's brandy sitting next to the
fireplace
That's what you mean to me

No choir, no solo, no symphony can sound as beautiful as your
whisper in my ear
When I think about you, I feel hurricanes move across oceans,
I feel mountains shake down into hills
I feel volcanoes burn into a fireplace
That's what I think about you

The Astral Realm Where Realities Collide

Relax your breath, take some time to enjoy a new wild ride
It's unfamiliar, crisp, new and full of spiritual potentialities
It's the astral realm where realities collide
Consider it as a parallel to your universe
The chance to see beyond the stars without the eulogy and the hearse
The sky is pink and the mountains glow with lavender streams
Your mind can fly, your soul can soar beyond your nightly dreams

Simply ground yourself through your root, the ancients call it your
red chakra
Connect back to the mother source, the one who flows like nur-
turing aqua
Steady your breath, clear your mind and eliminate the noise
Allow the living spirit within you to bridge the gap between the
worlds, the space that divinity employs
At times you may only hear quiet and peace around you like a glove
But eventually you will enter the astral realm where there are no
boundaries or carnal frailties
Introduce yourself to the real you who is guided by ancestral light
and divine synchronicities

Relax your breath, take some time to enjoy a new wild ride
Simultaneously it is not far, but still a million light years away
A spiritual escape where wisdom, guidance and peace are maintained
No airfare needed, no bags to pack, everything you need is inside
Welcome to the Astral Realm where Realities Collide

Softer Side of Summer

Let me love you like the softer side of summer
When the weather isn't hot and you wonder if you should go out
early or late
It's the type of love where you go to the beach in May
The ocean comes and the waves go in and out
It's that type of love that makes you want to lay out in the sun
while the kids around you shout
Beach balls in the air, volleyball playin', people running up and
down the beach, tossin' up the sand
Ain't this the beauty, the softer side of summer
It's that September and October flow, when it's not too hot and
it's not too cold
It's the months where you know your soul has control
No sweat glands in the process of producing
No chill is in the air
Just you and the softer side of summer everywhere
It's how you feel when you see her walk in and out of that store
with those autumn colors on
Remember, it's the softer side of summer
So when you see that glow that goes down deep to her very bones
Or when you look at him and see those shoulders perched back
and you know that he is strong
Remember you won't go wrong with the softer side of summer
You also have to understand
In order for GOD to create man
HE had to see the stronger side of summer
But when HE produced woman, HE envisioned and created the
softer side of summer

Together all seasons flow

It's just the softer side of summer that makes you lose control

Twinkle Twinkle Hershey Bars

Twinkle Twinkle Hershey Bars
How I like to drive expensive cars
Move away from my momma very far, land on a planet called Mars
When I get lonely I shoot for the stars
Scream Hallelujah as I come crashing down

Sitting back dreaming of a crown, only to get the most precious stones
My mom and dad's letdowns, my sisters' and brothers' hand-me-downs
Nothing but dental work, root canals and crowns

The funny thing about all this is it's no joke
If you live long enough, you're gonna pull one of these strings or
better yet a rope
A person with no hope is like a dope fiend with no dope
And if you can't understand this then you cannot cope
Twinkle Twinkle Hershey Bars
How I like to drive expensive cars
So I decide to put in work, persevere and set myself up until it's
for me

Where Can I Find Myself

Where Can I Find Myself?
Underneath the smile that lies?
Lies to impress the gaze of others?
Lies to soothe the hot breeze of contempt that I feel when they
walk by?

Where Can I Find Myself?
Behind the lustful murmurs of lovers past?
Behind the motives that shield my actions in cloudy insecurities?

Where Can I Find Myself?
Does she walk among the shattered pieces of shattered dreams?
Or dance beneath the ancient stones of ancestral shame?

Where Can I Find Myself?
Hidden between the misfortunes of past guilt and abuse?
Disguised by emotional ruins like depression and doubt?

Where Can I Find Myself?
Because she is lost, trapped, wanting to be free
Imprisoned by her own walls of hurt, pain and failure
Held captive by yesterday, gripped tight by my chains, waiting for
the captor to finally let her free,
When all along, the captor was me.

Needed Me

You needed me
Just like blood is so important to the veins
To everything inside and out
A stable brain is more important to the mind
Of the one that knows what is needed
Growth, seasons change and even though you know, you still seek
and search out
Because you need to know more
More, that certain feeling you yearn for
More, that certain desire you burn for
More, you need it, because it's an unanswered question
What is, who is and what about, all questions of needing with no doubt
Needing is an answer that you must chase
Because on every obstacle you still need HIM, but you've never
seen HIS face
You felt HIS warm arms, you felt HIS loving hands
You felt HIS kind SPIRIT, you felt it even when you thought you
were alone
You thought you would fall but yet you stand
Needed me and I am in HIM
We flow together like a waterfall
That you can't see because the little kids play in the rivers, in the
ponds and you watch them while they swim
Even though the ditches beside the road don't seem important
It's still a needing process to keep the land from being flooded
You need me like I need you
I'M like a lonely father searching for a child that was kidnapped
You can stop my search by answering, say I need YOU too

Lions and Tigers and Bears

I'm not afraid of lions and tigers and bears,
It's you that I'm afraid of
You that I'm scared of
You, with no personality or gender
It's you that I'm scared of
Love, I call your name even when I'm ashamed
Of the way you make me act
I call your name because I know deep down inside you feel my pain
You broke my heart, I gave you my all and you ripped it apart
But now I know, I understand the lyrical flow
I'm not afraid of lions and tigers and bears,
It's you that I'm afraid of
You that I'm scared of
I gave you the best of my love and you gave me nothing back
Nothing but late hours in the morning and sleepless nights
The thoughts of where you could be, and who you were with
Still wondering, still seeking, still looking for you when you forgot
about me
And all I did was love you
The most beautiful monsters in the world are the ones we choose
to love
The demons, that's that evil, the people that don't consider your heart
They just move through this world and shove by force, moving
people in and out of their lives
I wanted you to be my wife, I wanted you to be my everything, I
wanted you to be my love
But instead, you're the one I'm scared of, the one I'm in fear of
You are the one that my parents warned me about

The old people said that you would hurt me, just wait and see
But me and my pride, me and my foolish ego
I didn't listen to anybody
It was so real, wish they could feel what I feel
But it all came crashing down block by block like Legos
I'm not afraid of lions and tigers and bears,
It's you that I'm afraid of
You that I'm scared of

The Flower Garden

Whoever thought a garden would grow on 102nd Street?
Never was no garden there before.
All they had was the corner stores and the carwash on 105th Street.
Pollution and smog circled every corner in a haze of regret and
mistakes

Who in the world put a garden in the ghetto??
Next to the barbershop and the shutdown gas station
The gas station that was robbed last year on Christmas Eve
So sad how all that went down.

How in the world did they get a garden in this neighborhood
Where the kids are assumed to be early convicts, a waste of human
potential
As soon as they take their first breath on this side of creation

Yet, there it is, a flower garden.
Full of all GOD's colors and potentialities
Waiting, watching, growing,
Not in spite of the pollution, noise and social degeneration, but
because of it.

Inner Visions

Inner visions in the heart
A void without love and peace
Incomprehensible waves of loss and confusion
Memories that entrap and devour

Inner visions in the mind
Holding on to traumatic struggles
That attack from within
Making it hard to see the light

Inner visions in the heart
Devastated by loss, guilt and shame
Sadness for the failures
That seem to shape and mold from within

Inner visions within me
Why have I been my own worst enemy?
Holding myself in contempt and malice

Inner visions within me
Refusing to allow me to overcome the hurt of old
To contaminate my growth

Laying down the reigns of personal sabotage
Inner visions which shape my soul
Reclaiming the power encapsulated within
Giving my soul the permission it needs

To Be
To Soar
To conquer
To transform

Inner visions of a new me

Forgiven
Empowered
Endowed
Restored

Inner visions of the real me

Sun

Oh, sun, warm me in the wintertime
When the chills are down my spine
I need you most in the wintertime
While the world is cold and the shadows of the police
hover over my soul
While the concrete beats with the used needles of a desperate people
Behind the steeples, I see young kids playing, looking and yelling
as cars pass by, that's my car, that's my car
Young little stars soon to be
How can we beat this concrete?

Oh, sunlight, how can you beat me and the concrete?
How can you force me to lay down on something so steep?
How can you force me to lay down on something so hard
While a man dressed in blue says he is only doing his job
How can my blood run down my nose?
How can my eye be swollen shut?
How can my black people stand there
and look like nobody gives a ****?
One minute passes by, the sunshine is on my face
Can I feel the warmth of your deep embrace?
Two minutes pass by, just let me feel the warmth
before the cold sets in
Three minutes pass by, missing the warmth of my mother and my
loved ones
Four minutes pass by and I start to enter a deep, dark place
Yearning for the sunlight to shine upon my face
Five minutes go by, still nobody fights for me,

they sit and watch while I die
Oh, sun, shine on me just this one time
Why isn't being so cold a crime?
The guilty always seem to walk free
Except for me for just simply having melanin.
Why kill me for simply trying to be something I was chosen to be
The dedication of the sun and me as two friends who go through
life together in harmony
Until something cuts us off and makes me lie on this dirty concrete
The needles, the hardness of it,
the knee pressed down deep into my neck
Six minutes pass by, still I can't forget.
Still asking the sun to shine on me
Seven minutes pass by,
might as well close my eyes and feel deep breaths
As I try to visualize the sun shining down on me
The warmth of when I was three
playing on the swings at the playground
The monkey bars, the sliding board, aw man
Eight minutes pass by, there it goes, my feet, they are cold
Still not a soul said one word
And the only thing I could do
and think about before my life is through
Is to ask the sun to shine down on me in this wintertime
While this man accuses me but yet, he commits the crime

I Am a Queen on All Accords

I am a queen on all accords,
I will defend my mind, body and soul.
My divinity you will not shatter,
Your opinions about my actions, they do not matter

I am a queen on all accords,
He will defend my mind, body and soul.
He is my king, you can rest assured,
To shelter and protect, there is no challenge that he will not endure.

I am a queen on all accords,
I will defend my mind, body and soul.
Never will I settle for less than what I deserve,
All obstacles will I face with a steady nerve.

I am a queen on all accords,
ABBA will defend my mind, body and soul.
HE is my battle ram, when I'm in need,
My fortress, my rock, an undying creed.

I am a queen on all accords,
We will defend my mind, body and soul.
Leave no doubt about my worth
As a rare, valuable diamond found deep within Mother Earth

You will not define me,
You will not defile me,

My dreams,

My hopes

All stand before me.

Untitled

A rider without a horse is a sad sight to see
But a horse without a rider is a beautiful rarity

Shadow Self

The watchful eyes of others bring out what we desire for others to see
The happy, bright and smiling side of our public personality
The one who shines, does everything right with money left to spare
The one with a million likes,
the latest fashion and friends who all seem to care
The one who gives to charity, has compassion and a loving spouse
With perfect children, well maintained, and they always share
their whereabouts

What about the side of you who creeps about at night?
Lying to manipulate, hide your deeds and trouble to excite
The one who harbors the lower side of energy
Like hatred, greed, malicious words or sibling jealousy
The one who gossips about friends and chastises neighbors
Who selfishly cheats and demeans them in an effort to defile their
labor

It's the darker you, the lower you who hides away in the shadows
Who takes your hurt, guilt and shame, all of your spiritual blows
The one who fights the battles that the mind can't muster
Who holds the metaphysical lines when the difficulties seem to cluster
The side of you that helps you to survive when the arrows are dealt
Let me introduce you to the lower you, the darker you, it's your
shadow self

Do not make the mistake of hiding it or pretending it doesn't exist
For like it or not eventually the carnal manifestations will persist
They will ooze and leak into the crevices

that you made for your beautiful places
And create loathsome energies that wreak havoc and leave your re-
ality with only minute traces
Of the shining perfect world that you pretended to inhabit so long ago
Instead take the light that shines and allow it to overflow

Into your good, into your bad, into your mediocre
Find the strength, the wisdom, the courage to become a spiritual
broker
To bridge the gaps, close the divide and synthesize your soul
In this manner you will take back your strength, shine a light and
finally become whole
Introduce yourself to the lower, darker side of you, where diffi-
culties are expressed
Expose your hurt, your shame and grief and free your shadow self.

Remarkable

This world is quite frankly, unmistakably remarkable
The rainbow mountains of China are truly a sight to behold
With alternating layers of orange, red and yellow hues that make
the heart feel unstoppable
Macho Picchu is a grand example of art and form which breathes
of great adventure foretold
And Bora Bora in French Polynesia is a tropical paradise
The majestic mountain views of Patagonia will make your heart
beat with the energy of Mother
The purple blooms and flowing trees of New Zealand will surely entice
Your heart, your soul, your inner child to once again connect to
Mother

HIS world is quite frankly, unmistakably undeniably remarkable
The breathtaking sand dunes of Namibia are exquisitely layered by
the wind
The black sand beaches of Japan makes you feel as though any-
thing were possible
The waterfalls of Argentina are a structural masterpiece using just
the right blend
Of reality and fantasy, an aesthetic and spiritual release
Who can forget the pyramids of Egypt, a historical dynasty which
still casts a long shadow
Consider the island of Madagascar, famous for its Avenue of the
Baobab trees
Or the Canadian Rockies and glacial lakes which were sourced
from the snow

This world is quite frankly, unmistakably remarkable
And while this world does not belong to us, we all belong to it, as
it all flowed from the one great source from whence we all were
sourced

Enjoy the beauty and marvel at the artistry which is rather impeccable
Feel the oneness which flows and frees without energy that is coerced
This world is quite frankly, unmistakably, undeniably remarkable
Let it live and breathe in you

Labor Light

Labor light
Labor light
Labor light
Shocking to my sight
About to be transported into a new world, coming in through a
tight space
Tight space
Tight space
My mother's energy surrounds me just like a cool breeze
Still can't help but feel just a little bit of apprehension and unease
There is now distance between me and my mother's womb
The place that feels like heaven, a hibiscus in full bloom
Labor light
Labor light
I'm surrounded by foreign energy from where I know not
The unfamiliarity and coldness has my mind besot
I recall that HE was born in a manger
But was his room filled up with so many strangers?
Labor light
Labor light
Yearning for the darkness that nourished me back then,
longing to reunite
Afraid to open my eyes and my soul to the exposure of the light
Labor light
Trauma from my first sight
If only I could speak and tell my mother
to please turn off this labor light.
Just then I see the COMFORTER,

 ✦

with an entirely different light
Which calms and nourishes, soothes and empowers and gives me
peace and delight

I Do

In a manner which can only be described as grand
A MAN so sweet and valiant to give HIS life to ask me for my hand
A courtship so spiritually intoxicating, the essence of and presence of unconditional agape
Where all my frailties and blemishes were accounted for despite the previous heartache
An immortal, testimonial love which conquered death and the grave
Was bestowed upon me, by one cataclysmic sacrifice by which the world was saved
HIS heart so pure, HIS mind so wise and tongue so fierce that HE made them cower in their own carnality
But yet so gentle, so sincere, and so divine that HE synthesized the bridge of life to overcome all earthly principalities

HE was here before the world began, a PREEXISTENT PRINCE, like manna from above
HE was immersed within the flowing waters, and the SPIRIT appeared symbolized by a white dove
While they mocked HIS title and position which was a supernatural inheritance
HE loved the world, HIS fellow man and gave us another chance
A HEAVENLY KING and HIGH PRIEST of royal bloodline flowed
There is none greater that we may call, HIS glory overflowed
HE gave it all and risked it all to serve us everyone
So that the world and its despair we might all overcome

Why would one so great and astonishing consider me?
Who often falls to sin so near an original propensity

An intersection of metaphysical perfection
compared to my transgressions
After years and years of failing miserably
despite all of my spiritual weapons
Yet HE loved me so that HE forgave them all
and adorned me with a crown
A crown of matrimony, of spiritual and everlasting life,
throughout the ages of renown
Which grants me all components of eternal life
I am so proud and so honored to be HIS chosen wife
So mystified and excited to join the community of believers
That will also accept and shine in the glow of spiritual husbandry
which flows farther and deeper
Than any love that could ever exist in our earthly form
It's like the barometric pressure that drops before the storm
It fills you up and wraps you up in the arms of destiny
Which destroys all forms of hurt, all guilt and shameful legacies
In a manner which can only be described as grand
A MAN so sweet and valiant to give HIS life to ask me for my hand
Is knocking at my door
So honored, so enamored to say evermore
I will, I do and yes to you the one which I adore
My KING, my PRINCE, my divine, mi amour

Momma, Don't Cry

Momma, don't cry
When her lover fades
As the pains of labor pulsate through her body, consuming her
and leaving her hurt, and betrayed.

Momma, don't cry
When she's all alone, the bills are due
And there's no one to hold her close and say I do.

Momma, don't cry
When the kids don't listen and act up in school,
When their grades are low and her ideals and principles, due to
circumstance are often overruled

Momma, don't cry
When the world looks down on her for trying to survive
When the kids complain because the poverty stains the backdrop
which makes it difficult to thrive

Momma, don't cry
When she wears the mask of happiness over and over again
But when she is alone she struggles within to keep the anger and
resentment contained

Momma, don't cry
When they get up and leave because
They are tired of her rules and ready to live although she put her
own life on pause

Momma, don't cry
But she counts every step as necessary
Covering them with a passion and energy that is legendary
She nurtures and corrects, sharing her compassion in the effort of
making them great
Giving them the very things she missed, spiritual inheritance from
a higher state
She puts every ounce of her being into molding and saving you.
So you can never repay or measure close to exceed the standards
that she requires of you
Momma, don't cry
'Cause she hustles hard, smiles through pain and does anything
Anything to make her children fly

Rage

Hard-pressed, rocking, creaks, sounds
Boards taking pressure from above and underneath there is no ground
Orphaned, ripped from my planet and I don't know who is around
Darkness, chains, people packed like sardines in a can
This can't be where I'm headed, this can't be
Many men, many women, many children stacked to the top, is this a ship?
Or a sea building?
Homeland, secure land, my land, brother land, sister land, motherland, I can't see no more
How can you rip me from something, from one seashore to another seashore
Set up my core, replace it with something else, made me forget about where I came from
And then stripped me of my wealth
You stripped me even of my health
I'm on the front step like your morning milk
You on top of me wearing me out like silk
You pressed me from the day that you brought me to your seashore
Till 2020, now the police have a new type of force
How that ship sounds with them creaks and them cracks
Is the same identical sounds of that whip and that strap
It's the same identical sound as the handcuffs and that gat
Now you want to know why my people fear
Do you really want to know why my people fear
It's the sound of how we came from where we were to where we are at
How we joke and share good laughter but when the sirens come, we feel out of sorts and even flustered

You said march in peace, we did that
How can you march in peace when we stood in peace on a ship
that took us from where we were to where we are at
Stripped us from our own pride, we are orphans inside
We came into a country that said, now you have a newfound
American pride
Put your fist down, put the chains up
Scream "Black lives matter" and yet time isn't up
It's still ticking and it's the same oppression
Slave ship from homeland to mental depression
Dying from broken hearts from being ripped apart from a country
That my eyes never gazed on because of that old ship that sailed
across the sea
The cracks and the crumbles of the pressure of what's beneath
Many drowned on this voyage
So stay vigilant and remember age
Has you inside and if you are inside of age
Then you will understand why the youth feel rage

Promises Unfold

You can wait a lifetime or two for someone
and their promises to unfold
Slowly watching the years roll by as the reel of your life is played
Watching your dreams dissolve and slowly dissipate
While you sit nearby
While they casually try

You can lose your zest for life, your caress for this life
Lose your navigational guide, your own insatiable pride
Hurting the ones who love you the most
While you sit nearby
While they casually try
And perpetually lie

You can watch your heart break and allow your soul to ache
While your purpose is defiled and your energy they take
While you abandon the covenants that your fathers made
While you sit nearby
While they casually try
And perpetually lie
Causing your flame to die

You can wait a lifetime or two for someone
and their promises to unfold
Or you can look to the sky,
follow your heart and uncover spiritual gold
Joy is the fullness of and the abundance of strength
in mind, body and soul

Give yourself a try
Don't sit casually by
Truly live before you die
Every day is your chance to fly

Please Stand Up

To the Navajo Nation:
Proud and true, jeered, cast down but not defeated
Let's take the time to celebrate you, congratulate you,
it's not the time to stay in your seat
Won't you put your hands up, for the coming together,
Won't you please stand up
Won't you please stand up

To the Cherokee Nation:
Warriors, healers, tribal chieftains and my cousins too
Through the hard times, and the lean times, almost destroyed
times, you are my brothers through and through
Won't you put your hands up for the coming together,
Won't you please stand up
Won't you please stand up

To my Latino community,
so spicy, so strong like the fire that burns
Let us embrace your spark and zest for this life,
your passion which yearns
Won't you put your hands up for the coming together,
Won't you please stand up
Won't you please stand up

To my African family,
the original man who built the pyramids and tamed the land
You flowered the world, survived a myriad of assaults
and still you stand

Won't you put your hands up for the coming together,
Won't you please stand up
Won't you please stand up

To my Puerto Rican and Haitian brothers
who shine like precious jewels
Who lifts the world up, lifts each other up,
using difficulties for fuel
Won't you put your hands up for the coming together,
Won't you please stand up
Won't you please stand up

To the beautiful people of Ecuador, Laos and Brazil
To the lovely ones of Italy, France and Australia too
To my brothers of Iran, Turkey, Greece and Peru
To America, Estonia, Botswana and the whole wide world
You are a striking image of HIS own hand,
designed with love to be unique like pearls
Yet strikingly the same, an image of,
the very semblance of the UNIVERSAL MAKER
So why not join hands, hearts and minds
to celebrate what's greater?
Won't you put your hands up for the coming together,
Won't you please stand up
Won't you please stand up
Now and not later 'cause time is almost up
Before we meet the SUPREME PLANETARY SHAKER
The UNIVERSAL MATCHMAKER

The GREAT ARCHITECT, the GOOD SHEPARD,
the SUPREME CARETAKER
Won't you put your hands up for the coming together,
Won't you please stand up
Won't you please stand up

Morning

Gentle dew that is on the ground
It's simple, it's light, it's wet and it's an action that occurs when
no one is around
Every city, every town and every countryside feels it
It's that warmth that lets you feel how it commits
Simple is sometimes the best way to show gratitude and love
With a showering mist which comes from above
Whether it be dew or sprinkling raindrops
It is the boundary that allows you to see where everything starts
and where everything stops
Peaking over the trees, the sun will rise
Going higher and higher until it reaches the peak of the skies
It shines bright and dries up all the dew
It shines bright and even shines on you
The spirit feels light and your heart feels the warm embrace
Yet in the heat of the day, you dare hide your face
When something bright like that is shining upon you
Embrace it for your life could be filled up with nothing but dew

Measuring Tape

When you find yourself in the mirror
standing next to the measuring tape
Take a moment and realize that you need to contemplate
Who or what is holding out the tape whose measurements
you have chosen to adopt
Unfortunately it is your own ideals and standards
you have given up to swap

What do you see as successful and worthy of acclaim
And is it based on your internal dialogue or a manufactured fantasy
What is your desired goal or must we all look the same
And whose perceptions and ideals have created your reality

When you consider beauty, what do you see?
Is it the caricature from magazines or movies that they conceptualize
Or the models chosen to perpetuate the ideals envisioned by society
Or can you see the spectacular beauty hidden deep within your
own two eyes

So when you stare in the mirror with the measuring tape
Make sure you take the time to really contemplate
Whether you are making adjustments based on your own inner wisdom
If not, then you are just another notch in the system

The Drumbeat of the People

Listen closely so you can hear
The Drumbeat of the People
Coming closer and closer still
With each passing moment
A pulsating sound, a swift steady thud
That is moving through the land
Listen up, 'cause you can't miss it
Its infectious energy
Demanding justice now,
Reform and liberation
Fists up for equality and morality
Listen up so you can hear
The Drumbeat of the People
Getting louder and closer every day
The balances are weighed for systematic equality
Justice now, liberation now, freedom for us all

Wanderer

The wanderer you see has walked through distant lands
Traveled over oceans and continents of a monumental span
Walked through the corridors of time as manifested to the soul
Intersected with chance and coincidence and counseled for control

The wanderer you see, is rarely seen or heard
Moving through dimensions most often undeterred
The purpose is unique and it is so grand, several evolutions
through the GREAT ONE'S hand
Growing and learning with each go-'round, increasing while the
cosmos expand

The wanderer you see is an evolving, moving replica of your DNA
To raise your vibration, your energy and to guide your way
Sometimes it appears in your mother's eyes or your uncle's laughter
But if you're not careful you will miss the nuggets left on your
hereafter

To help you spin your center back to the starting point
To the origin of evermore, the universal flashpoint
The wanderer moves through time, reality and your consciousness
Make sure you pay attention and listen up with all confidence
For the wanderer who comes though, the wanderer who is the es-
sence of you

Life

To find happiness, one has to first go through pain
My pain made me dull but my self-happiness made me live again
Because no one should depend on anyone else for happiness in life
Life is to be lived in fulfillment of embracing new adventures and
learning new ways to love

The Warmth of Love

When all the memories fail and life faints
I look to you to grab my hand and help me paint
As my hands get weak and I need a guide
I hold true to the light that burns inside
As the light begins to get faint and fade
I remember that your love is as beautiful as the everglades
As the darkness sets in as tomorrow is not promised
I see that what I had will be never be forgotten
From a love that is untold
From the sheer beauty of you washing clothes
Knowing that I am in love with you
If there ever were a heart stone, it would be whatever color you
choose it to be
I am what I am because of you
My days grow longer and the nights grow colder
Because what's in front of me is the size of a boulder
As I roll the stone away and gasp at my tomb
I remember the warmth of love and what I left inside your womb

Star Gazing

Two lovers walking in the night
Gazing at the stars wondering why they are so bright
They don't know that on this night, this man has found his wife
The stars came together perfectly for this one night
No need for a sweet sultry love song, the universe has swallowed
these two in her forever belly
Darkness gives birth to light and love has been shown
The greatest love I have found is the greatest love that has always
been known
When I made you, I knew who you were in the womb
MY plans to prosper you and how
You heard the fairytales of the cow who jumped over the moon
And slaves who jumped over the broom
The way you get scared every time you hear that thunder clash and
you hear that loud boom
Is the same love that you find in your lover at night
Can't trust his hands 'cause they are not even in sight
His pride in knowing that he will not give up the fight
And if anything happens in the middle of the night, he will be the
one to get up and grab that flashlight
Two lovers gazing, walking in the night
Gazing up at the stars, wondering why they are so bright
On this night that man has a woman locked in his sights
Something so beautiful, doing what GOD commanded, he found
himself a wife

I Hate It But I Love Him

I hate it but I love him
Naw, it ain't perfect
When I get inside my feelings, I'm like a reject
I'm like the people on the island in the Santa Claus movie, I'm a
perfect misfit
I don't like it so I quit
Put me on an island by myself and don't you try to come to it
For if you do you will see, I don't really like you but I love you
I'm confused, I'm a hurt little boy who needs someone to guide me
But instead I fight me
Because I know nobody likes me and I won't let them love me
So what I do is shove them really hard until I remove them from me
Instead of trying to be perfect
I would rather infect
And make them reject
The energy that I'm trying to brew
'Cause I don't like saying the words I love you
My love came with a cost
It hurt when I lost
My dad introduced me to the deepest hurt I ever had
I introduced him to my daughter
But the relationship between dad and son was still loose
I brought my daughter here to tighten us up like a noose
To let you know that you have a granddaughter and I'm counting
on you to see me as a man
But you act like you are sinking in quicksand
Daddy, quit moving, stop swimming, you're gonna sink faster, man
Before I know it, you are going down in the ground

Now all of that love and hatred, I keep it bound up
In my heart
Tearing my family up like plastic cups
Ripping them apart

Ancestors

Sweet, sweet Chinese

Made that black man fall down on his knees

To ask that sweet, beautiful woman named Chinese

To trust enough to accept and marry me

Set my poor soul at ease, set my soul free

With your love

For you are as black and as beautiful as a white dove

You are as strong as leather

Let me show you that I will walk with you through any weather

I will shield you from the rain

Hide you from your pain

And if anything goes wrong, I promise you my love will never change

What he said, he meant

Words hardly got spent

Money, yeah, he always lent

But the factor is, can you honor him?

Can you really honor him?

Can you honor the uncles and aunts that walked before you?

The ones that lay down before you

The ones that went in the ground before you?

Can you honor Sonny, can you honor Charles

Can you honor Mary, can you honor Martha?

Can you honor them all?

Can you honor Beth, can you honor Gloria

For her story has been told

Didn't it catch a part of you?

How strong was Chinese to make her daughters strong, independent women?

When you always sat back and wondered
How can love be that tough and still love enough?
The tombstones will fade
The sun has no shade
Honor your ancestors, don't let them go down alone in the cold,
cold ground
For they are always around

www.ingramcontent.com/pod-product-compliance
Lightning Source LLC
Chambersburg PA
CBHW051008060726
47593CB00017B/1268